# France

## by Cynthia Klingel
## and Robert B. Noyed

Content Adviser: Arnold Ages, Ph.D.,
Department of French Studies,
The University of Waterloo, Ontario

Social Science Adviser: Professor Sherry L. Field,
Department of Curriculum and Instruction, College of Education,
The University of Texas at Austin

Reading Adviser: Dr. Linda D. Labbo,
Department of Reading Education, College of Education,
The University of Georgia

**COMPASS POINT BOOKS**

Minneapolis, Minnesota

FIRST REPORTS

Compass Point Books
3722 West 50th Street, #115
Minneapolis, MN 55410

Visit Compass Point Books on the Internet at *www.compasspointbooks.com* or e-mail your request to *custserv@compasspointbooks.com*

Cover: Eiffel Tower in Paris, France

Photographs ©: Reuters/Langsdon/Hulton Getty/Archive Photos, cover; Photo Network/Chad Ehlers, 4, 30-31; Trip/H. Rogers, 6-7, 22, 23, 24; Spencer Swanger/Tom Stack & Associates, 8; Photo Network/Stephen Saks, 9; Trip/D. Houghton, 10; Trip/T. Bognar, 11; North Wind Picture Archives, 12, 13, 14, 15; Reuters/Jack Dabaghian/Hulton Getty/Archive Photos, 16; Trip/S. Grant, 17; Reuters/Jacky Naegelen/Hulton Getty/Archive Photos, 18; Hal Beral/Visuals Unlimited, 19; Trip/Eric Smith, 20; R. J. Goldstein/Visuals Unlimited, 21; Reuters/Stefano Rellandini/Hulton Getty/Archive Photos, 25; Trip/N. Ray, 26; Reuters/Eric Gaillard/Hulton Getty/Archive Photos, 27; Photophile/Bachmann, 28; Gianni Dagli Orti/Corbis, 29; Hulton Getty/Archive Photos, 32; Trip/Chris Parker, 34; Trip/D. Palais, 35; Trip/D. Hastilow, 36; Robert Fried/Tom Stack & Associates, 37; Digital Stock, 38-39, 40-41, 43; Unicorn Stock Photos/Florent Flipper, 42; J. C. Carton/European Central Bank/Bruce Coleman Inc., 45.

Editors: E. Russell Primm, Emily J. Dolbear, and Neal Durando
Photo Researchers: Svetlana Zhurkina and Jo Miller
Photo Selector: Catherine Neitge
Designer: Bradfordesign, Inc.
Cartographer: XNR Productions, Inc.

**Library of Congress Cataloging-in-Publication Data**
Klingel, Cynthia Fitterer.
    France / by Cynthia Klingel and Robert Noyed.
        p. cm. — (First reports)
    Includes bibliographical references and index.
    Summary: An introduction to the geography, history, culture, and people of the largest country in western Europe.
    ISBN 0-7565-0184-9
    1. France—Juvenile literature. [1. France.] I. Noyed, Robert B. II. Title. III. Series.
    DC17 .K55 2002
944—dc21                                                             2001004373

# Table of Contents

# "Bonjour!"

△ *Two schoolgirls walk through a vineyard in Bordeaux.*

"*Bonjour* and welcome to France!" *Bonjour* means "hello" in French.

If you visit France, you will see many beautiful buildings and fine works of art. You might eat some tasty foods, too. You may attend a concert, a ballet, or a

▲ *Map of France*

soccer game. Or maybe you'd like to travel to the
ocean or the mountains and large forests of France.

5

Paris is France's capital and largest city.

France is the biggest country in western Europe. It is almost as big as the state of Texas. More than 59 million people live in France.

France touches eight countries. Belgium, Luxembourg, and Germany lie northeast of France. Switzerland and Italy are on the east. Spain, Andorra, and Monaco lie south of France.

Three important bodies of water touch the borders of France. The English Channel is to the north. The Atlantic Ocean is to the west. The Mediterranean Sea is to the south.

Paris is the capital of France. It is also France's largest city.

# Land in France

France has three mountain ranges. The Alps and the Jura Mountains are in the east. Mont Blanc, the tallest mountain in western Europe, is in the French Alps. The Pyrenees are in the southwest. The mountains are cold and covered with snow in the winter.

△ Mount Blanc is the tallest mountain in western Europe.

▲ *The Pyrenees are in southwest France.*

North and central France are low and flat. Thick forests cover parts of central France. These forests get more rain than the rest of the country. Many plants and animals can be found here.

Part of this area is called the highland **plateau**. It is hard to live here because of the steep and rocky hills.

△ *The rocky cliffs of Brittany*

The weather here is stormy in summer and cold in winter.

France has many rivers. The longest river in France is the Loire River. It is about 650 miles (1,046 kilometers) long. Other large rivers in France are the Seine, Rhône, Garonne, and Rhine.

France has more than 2,000 miles (3,218 kilometers) of coastline. The north coast is famous for its beautiful cliffs and beaches.

▲ *Swimmers and sunbathers enjoy the beaches on the Mediterranean Sea near Nice.*

The coast in the south is rocky. However, the southern coast is the warmest part of France. It is hot in the summer and mild in winter.

# History of France

The Gauls of ancient France fought against the Roman invaders.

The first people who lived in France were called the Gauls. About 2,000 years ago, Roman **invaders** arrived in France. They fought the Gauls and won.

Later, tribes from the east moved to France. One of these tribes was called the Franks. The name *France* comes from this group of people.

By the year 800, the **emperor** named

Charlemagne ruled France. He was a great ruler. He made France into a strong and powerful country.

After Charlemagne died, many kings ruled France. Over time, the French people grew unhappy. They

▲ *Charlemagne was a great ruler.*

△ *The royal palace was attacked during the French Revolution.*

wanted a new kind of government. In 1789, they fought the king's army and won. This war was called the French Revolution.

Napoléon Bonaparte was one of the new leaders of the French **Republic**. He became a famous general in world history. Napoléon also changed the way France was run. He made the government strong.

▲ *Napoléon Bonaparte*

△ *The French parliament*

Today, France's government has a president and a prime minister. The president is chosen by the people of France. The president then chooses a prime minister. Both of them work with **parliament** to run the country.

▲ *Citroën vehicles are made in France.*

France has many important businesses and industries. Many products made in France are sold in other countries. This practice is called **exporting**. Only three other countries in the world export more goods than France.

Coal, iron, petroleum, and natural gas are all

found in France. Coal and natural gas help make electricity. Iron and other materials are used to make products such as cars, airplanes, trucks, and ships. The cloth and perfume from France are also sold around the world.

Farming is a big business in France, too. Many farms grow grapes that are made into wine. France makes more wine than any other country in the world.

△ Jean-Paul Guerlain, a perfume creator, tests a new range of smells in his Paris lab.

▲ *Fields of sunflowers bloom in the Loire Valley.*

Sunflowers grown in France are used to make cooking oils. Other crops are wheat, barley, and sugar beets. Livestock such as chickens and cows are also raised in France.

△ *Fashion is big business in France.*

Another big business in France is the fashion industry. Paris is sometimes called "the fashion capital of the world." Many different styles of clothing are made in France.

# Life in France

French people are proud of their language. Most people who live in France were born there. But some French people were born in Algeria, Portugal, Africa, Italy, Morocco, and Turkey.

Most French people live in or near cities. Very few

▲ *Most people live in or near cities, such as Avignon, where these residents enjoy an outdoor café.*

French people live in the country or in a village. Most French people are Roman Catholic.

French families, including aunts, uncles, cousins, and grandparents, are very close. The parents know that raising children is an important responsibility.

French families also love pets. Most families in France have at least one pet.

△ *French teenagers listen to music at a park.*

▲ *French students at school*

French children are expected to study hard in school and at home. Most French children start school when they are only three years old. Parents expect their children to get good grades.

French people like to relax. At home, they read books and watch television. They also go to movies, concerts, plays, and museums. Some French people enjoy fishing, gardening, and hiking.

△ *The Centre Georges Pompidou is a modern art museum in Paris.*

Soccer is a favorite team sport. Skiing, tennis, rugby, and bicycling are also popular.

France is famous for its *Tour de France*, a bicycle race held each summer. The race is hundreds of miles long and passes through several countries.

▲ A pack of bicycle riders makes its way past a church
near Revel during the Tour de France.

# Holidays

French people enjoy celebrating many holidays. Some holidays, such as Christmas and Easter, are celebrated much as they are in the United States. In France, Christmas is called *Noel.*

Another special holiday is called *Mardi Gras.* In English, *Mardi Gras* means "Fat Tuesday." Mardi Gras

△ *A Mardi Gras parade in Nice*

▲ *Military jets fly over the Arc de Triomphe in Paris during a Bastille Day celebration.*

is held on the Tuesday before Lent begins. People wear costumes and parade through the streets. They also attend parties.

Another special French holiday is Bastille Day, on July 14. This day celebrates the French Revolution in 1789. Bastille Day is very much like the Fourth of July in the United States. People in France set off fireworks and attend dances and parties on Bastille Day.

# The Arts

The arts are important to the people of France. The arts include dance, theater, painting, sculpture, music, and writing. The French think the arts are among the best things of life.

△ *The Louvre is the largest art museum in France.*

France has many museums. The largest art museum is the Louvre in Paris. One of the most famous paintings in the Louvre is the *Mona Lisa*. Leonardo da Vinci painted the *Mona Lisa* in 1503.

◀ Mona Lisa *by Leonardo da Vinci*

△ *The Paris Opéra opened in 1875.*

Many of the world's most famous artists and writers lived and worked in France. Claude Monet, Pierre Auguste Renoir, and Henri Matisse are three well-known French artists. Famous French writers include Gustave Flaubert, Albert Camus, and Marguerite Duras.

The French are also known for designing beautiful buildings. Many of their buildings are seen as works of art. Many are hundreds of years old.

*Auguste, left, and Louis Lumière invented the first movie camera in the 1890s.*

Movies and films are popular in France. Louis and Auguste Lumière invented the first movie camera in France in the late 1800s. The Cannes International Film Festival is held each year in southern France. Famous people and movie stars from many countries attend the festival.

# French Food

The French enjoy cooking and eating fine food. People around the world enjoy the cooking style of French chefs.

One famous cooking style is *haute cuisine*. This is a fancy kind of cooking created for wealthy people. But soon, people everywhere were cooking food this way. These foods are rich and taste delicious. They often have thick sauces or fillings of cheese, vegetables, and seafood.

French bread is made in bakeries around the world. It comes in long, skinny loaves. This bread is crusty on the outside and fluffy inside.

French wine is also famous everywhere. Some of the best wine in the world is made in France. In France, wine is often served at lunch and dinner.

Eating is a time to relax in France. Meals are served and eaten slowly. The French eat three meals a day.

△ *A young girl carries long, skinny loaves of French bread.*

The first meal is breakfast, called *le petit déjeuner*.
This light meal is often a soft roll called a *croissant*
and coffee or hot chocolate.

▲ *The French usually have coffee and a croissant for breakfast.*

△ *Food served for dinner is beautifully arranged.*

The noon meal, called *le déjeuner*, used to be the main meal of the day. Now, the evening meal, or *le dîner*, is often the main meal. At this meal, various dishes are served separately. The meal is served in five courses. Visitors love the wonderful meals served in France.

# Paris—The Capital

Paris is the capital and largest city in France. More than 2 million people live in the city of Paris. Some 14 million live in and around Paris.

Paris was first built on an island in the middle of the Seine River more than 2,000 years ago. The first

▲ *The Arc de Triomphe is at the end of Avenue des Champs-Élysées in Paris.*

△ *The Eiffel Tower is a famous Paris landmark.*

people living in Paris were fishermen. Today, that island is only a small part of the entire city.

The Eiffel Tower, or *Tour Eiffel* as it is called in French, is also in Paris. It was built in 1889 for the World's Fair. Visitors can take an elevator to the top of the tower. It is very tall. They can see for 50 miles (80 kilometers) from the top of the tower.

The Cathedral of Notre Dame is another very famous landmark in Paris. It took almost 200 years to build Notre Dame. It was finished in 1250. Notre Dame is one of the most beautiful churches in the world.

Paris is often called "the City of Lights." Its many beautiful buildings are lit up at night. The dazzling display of thousands of lights earned the French capital its nickname.

▲ *Notre Dame is one of the most beautiful churches in the world.*

# France Today

Its long and interesting history makes France a wonderful place to visit. The art, food, buildings, and scenic beauty of France attract many visitors.

France's business and industry are also important. Food and other products from France are sold throughout the world.

France is a strong and successful country. Its

△ *In France, visitors and residents travel on high-speed trains.*

▲ *Mont-Saint-Michel in northern France is a popular tourist attraction.*

people have many reasons to be proud. When you leave France, you might say, "*Au revoir*—see you later, France!"

## Glossary

**emperor**—a male ruler of a group of countries or territories

**exporting**—selling products to other countries

**invaders**—armed forces that go into a country to take it over

**parliament**—a group of people who are elected to make laws

**plateau**—a high, flat land

**republic**—a country whose people vote for their leaders

## Did You Know?

• Paris was founded in 52 B.C.

• After the Eiffel Tower was built for the World's Fair in 1889, the people of Paris wanted to take it down, but it was too expensive.

• The Louvre has about 8 miles (13 kilometers) of galleries.

• France makes about 1.6 billion gallons (6 billion liters) of wine a year.

## At a Glance

**Official name:** French Republic

**Capital:** Paris

**Official language:** French

**National song:** "La Marseillaise"

**Area:** 212,918 square miles (551,458 square kilometers)

**Highest point:** Mont Blanc, 15,771 feet (4,810 meters)

**Lowest point:** Rhône River Delta, slightly below sea level

**Population:** 59,329,691 (2000 estimate)

**Head of government:** Prime minister

**Money:** Euro

# Important Dates

| | |
|---|---|
| **A.D. 200s** | The Franks begin settling in the area now known as France. |
| **800** | Emperor Charlemagne rules France. |
| **1250** | Notre Dame Cathedral is completed. |
| **1682** | Louis XIV moves the French court to Versailles. |
| **1789** | The people of France begin the French Revolution. |
| **1804** | Napoléon Bonaparte declares himself emperor of France. |
| **1889** | The Eiffel Tower is completed. |
| **1939–1945** | World War II is fought. |
| **1940** | German troops invade France. |
| **1962** | France gives Algeria independence after a long civil war. |
| **1993** | France helps form the European Union. |
| **1994** | Workers complete a tunnel under the English Channel linking France and Great Britain. |
| **2002** | The euro replaces the French franc on January 1. |

## Want to Know More?

### At the Library

Conboy, Fiona. *Welcome to France*. Milwaukee, Wis.: Gareth Stevens Publishing, 2000.

Nickles, Greg. *France: The People*. New York: Crabtree, 2000.

Powell, Jillian. *A History of France Through Art*. New York: Thomson Learning, 1996.

Ross, Stewart. *The Fall of the Bastille: Revolution in France*. Chicago: Heinemann Library, 2001.

### On the Web

**Factmonster Almanac**
*http://www.factmonster.com/ipka/A0107517.html*
For more information about the geography and history of France

**The French Embassy**
*http://www.ambafrance-us.org/kids/*
For information about life in France, plus games and more

### Through the Mail

**Tourisme Québec**
C.P. 979
Montreal, Quebec H3C 2W3
Canada
To learn more about French culture in Canada

### On the Road

**Sterling and Francine Clark Art Institute**
225 South Street
Williamstown, MA 01267
413/458-2303
To see this museum's extraordinary collection of French Impressionist paintings

# Index

**About the Authors**

Cynthia Klingel has worked as a high school English teacher and an elementary school teacher. She is currently the curriculum director for a Minnesota school district. Cynthia Klingel lives with her family in Mankato, Minnesota.

Robert B. Noyed started his career as a newspaper reporter. Since then, he has worked in school communications and public relations at the state and national level. Robert B. Noyed lives with his family in Brooklyn Center, Minnesota.